PRAYER BEFORE A CRUCIFIX

Look down upon me, good and gentle Jesus, while I kneel and ask You to fill my heart with faith, hope, charity and true sorrow for my sins. Help me never to sin again.

I think of Your five wounds with great love and pity as I repeat the words of Your prophet, David, "They have pierced my hands and my feet; they have injured all my bones."

(Say one Our Father, Hail Mary, and Glory Be, for the Pope.)

" I will be with you all Days,

....

received

The Body of Christ for the First Time

on ....

at ....

.... *Pastor*

Even until the End of time. "

May the Blessed Mother keep under her special care the boys and the girls who learn to love her Son better by using this Mass Book.

marian
CHILDREN'S MASS BOOK

Written By
Sister Mary Theola, s.s.n.d.

Edited By
Rev. Victor Hoagland, C.P.

Illustrated By
George Angelini

Regina
Press

Dedication

First published in 1952, the Marian Children's Mass Book is one of the most popular Communion books ever published. Over the years it has been translated into 14 languages. This, the newly revised sixth edition, is dedicated to Charles, Edmond and George Malhame, our Grandfather, Father and Uncle, whose contributions were instrumental to its success.

George and Robert

Nihil Obstat: Reverend Monsignor Joseph DeGrocco
Censor Librorum
November 15, 2011

Imprimatur: Most Reverend William Murphy
Bishop of Rockville Centre
November 16, 2011

Published with the approval of the Committee on Divine Worship of the United States Conference of Catholic Bishops.

CPSIA July 2025 10 9 8 7 6 5 L/P

Printed in China.

CONTENTS

THE ORDER OF MASS

THE INTRODUCTORY RITES

When he has arrived at the altar, after making a profound bow with the ministers, the Priest venerates the altar with a kiss and, if appropriate, incenses the cross and the altar. Then, with the ministers, he goes to the chair. When the Entrance Chant is concluded, the Priest and the faithful, standing, sign themselves with the Sign of the Cross, while the Priest, facing the people, says:

Priest: **In the name of the Father, and of the Son, and of the Holy Spirit.**

People: **Amen.**

Then the Priest, extending his hands, greets the people, saying:

Priest: **The grace of our Lord Jesus Christ,**
and the love of God,
and the communion of the Holy Spirit
be with you all.

People: **And with your spirit.**

Or:

Priest: **Grace to you and peace from God our Father and the Lord Jesus Christ.**

People: **And with your spirit.**

Or:

Priest: **The Lord be with you.**

In this first greeting a Bishop, instead of The Lord be with you, says:

Bishop: **Peace be with you.**

People: **And with your spirit.**

PENITENTIAL ACT

Then follows the Penitential Act, to which the Priest invites the faithful, saying:

Priest:

Brethren (brothers and sisters),
let us acknowledge our sins,
and so prepare ourselves to celebrate
the sacred mysteries.

A brief pause for silence follows. Then all recite together the formula of general confession:

Priest and People:

I confess to almighty God
and to you, my brothers and sisters,
that I have greatly sinned,
in my thoughts and in my words,
in what I have done and in what I have failed to do,

And, striking their breast, they say:

through my fault, through my fault,
through my most grievous fault;

Then they continue:

therefore I ask blessed Mary ever-Virgin,
all the Angels and Saints,
and you, my brothers and sisters,
to pray for me to the Lord our God.

Or:

Priest: **Have mercy on us, O Lord.**
People: **For we have sinned against you.**
Priest: **Show us, O Lord, your mercy.**
People: **And grant us your salvation.**

Or:

The Priest, or a Deacon or another minister:
You were sent to heal the contrite of heart:
Lord, have mercy. Or: **Kyrie, eleison.**
People: **Lord, have mercy.** Or: **Kyrie, eleison.**

Or:

The Priest, or a Deacon or another minister:
You came to call sinners:
Christ, have mercy. Or: **Christe, eleison.**
People: **Christ, have mercy.** Or: **Christe, eleison.**

Or:

The Priest, or a Deacon or another minister:
You are seated at the right hand
of the Father to intercede for us:
Lord, have mercy. Or: **Kyrie, eleison.**
People: **Lord, have mercy.** Or: **Kyrie, eleison.**

ABSOLUTION

Priest: **May almighty God have mercy on us,**
forgive us our sins,
and bring us to everlasting life.

People: **Amen.**

The Kyrie, eleison (Lord, have mercy) invocations follow, unless they have just occurred in a formula of the Penitential Act.

V. **Lord, have mercy.** R. **Lord, have mercy.**
V. **Christ, have mercy.** R. **Christ, have mercy.**
V. **Lord, have mercy.** R. **Lord, have mercy.**

Or:

V. **Kyrie, eleison.** R. **Kyrie, eleison.**
V. **Christe, eleison.** R. **Christe, eleison.**
V. **Kyrie, eleison.** R. **Kyrie, eleison.**

GLORIA

Glory to God in the highest,
and on earth peace to people of good will.

We praise you,
we bless you,
we adore you,
we glorify you,
we give you thanks for your great glory,
Lord God, heavenly King,
O God, almighty Father.

Lord Jesus Christ, Only Begotten Son,
Lord God, Lamb of God, Son of the Father,
you take away the sins of the world,
    have mercy on us;
you take away the sins of the world,
    receive our prayer;
you are seated at the right hand of the Father,
    have mercy on us.

For you alone are the Holy One,
you alone are the Lord,

you alone are the Most High,
Jesus Christ,
with the Holy Spirit,
in the glory of God the Father.
Amen.

When this hymn is concluded, the Priest, with hands joined, says:

Priest: **Let us pray.**

And all pray in silence with the Priest for a while.

Then the Priest, with hands extended, says the Collect prayer, at the end of which the people acclaim:

People: **Amen.**

THE LITURGY OF THE WORD

FIRST READING

Then the reader goes to the ambo and reads the First Reading, while all sit and listen. To indicate the end of the reading, the reader acclaims:

Reader: **The word of the Lord.**

People: **Thanks be to God.**

The psalmist or cantor sings or says the Psalm, with the people making the response.

SECOND READING

After this, if there is to be a Second Reading, a reader reads it from the ambo, as above.

To indicate the end of the reading, the reader acclaims:

Reader: **The word of the Lord.**

People: **Thanks be to God.**

GOSPEL DIALOGUE

There follows the Alleluia or another chant laid down by the rubrics, as the liturgical time requires.

Deacon or Priest: **The Lord be with you.**

People: **And with your spirit.**

The Deacon, or the Priest:

A reading from the holy Gospel according to N.

and, at the same time, he makes the Sign of the Cross on the book and on his forehead, lips, and breast.

People: **Glory to you, O Lord.**

At the end of the Gospel:

Deacon, or the Priest:

The Gospel of the Lord.

People: **Praise to you, Lord Jesus Christ.**

Then follows the Homily, which is to be preached by a Priest or Deacon on all Sundays and Holydays of Obligation; on other days, it is recommended.

At the end of the Homily, the Symbol or Profession of Faith or Creed, when prescribed, is either sung or said:

PROFESSION OF FAITH OR CREED

I believe in one God,
the Father almighty,
maker of heaven and earth,
of all things visible and invisible.

I believe in one Lord Jesus Christ,
the Only Begotten Son of God,
born of the Father before all ages.
God from God, Light from Light,
true God from true God,
begotten, not made, consubstantial with the Father;
through him all things were made.
For us men and for our salvation
he came down from heaven,

At the words that follow, up to and including and became man, all bow.

and by the Holy Spirit was incarnate of the Virgin Mary,
and became man.

For our sake he was crucified under Pontius Pilate,
he suffered death and was buried,
and rose again on the third day

in accordance with the Scriptures.
He ascended into heaven
and is seated at the right hand of the Father.
He will come again in glory
to judge the living and the dead
and his kingdom will have no end.

I believe in the Holy Spirit, the Lord, the giver of life,
who proceeds from the Father and the Son,
who with the Father and the Son
is adored and glorified,
who has spoken through the prophets.

I believe in one, holy, catholic and apostolic Church.
I confess one Baptism for the forgiveness of sins
and I look forward to the resurrection of the dead
and the life of the world to come. Amen.

Instead of the Niceno-Constantinopolitan Creed, especially during Lent and Easter Time,
the baptismal Symbol of the Roman Church, known as the Apostles' Creed, may be used.

I believe in God,
the Father almighty,

Creator of heaven and earth,
and in Jesus Christ, his only Son, our Lord,

At the words that follow, up to and including the Virgin Mary, *all bow.*

who was conceived by the Holy Spirit,
born of the Virgin Mary,
suffered under Pontius Pilate,
was crucified, died and was buried;
he descended into hell;
on the third day he rose again from the dead;
he ascended into heaven,
and is seated at the right hand of God the Father almighty;
from there he will come to judge the living
and the dead.

I believe in the Holy Spirit,
the holy catholic Church,
the communion of saints,
the forgiveness of sins,
the resurrection of the body,
and life everlasting. Amen.

THE LITURGY OF THE EUCHARIST

PRESENTATION AND PREPARATION OF THE GIFTS

It is desirable that the faithful express their participation by making an offering, bringing forward bread and wine for the celebration of the Eucharist and perhaps other gifts to relieve the needs of the Church and of the poor.

Priest: **Blessed are you, Lord**
God of all creation,
for through your goodness
we have received
the bread we offer you:
fruit of the earth and work
of human hands,
it will become for us
the bread of life.

Then he places the paten with the bread on the corporal. If, however, the Offertory Chant is not sung, the Priest may speak these words aloud; at the end, the people may acclaim:

People: **Blessed be God for ever.**

Priest: **Blessed are you, Lord God of all creation,**
for through your goodness we have received
the wine we offer you:

fruit of the vine and work of human hands,
it will become our spiritual drink.

People: **Blessed be God for ever.**

INVITATION TO PRAYER

Standing at the middle of the altar, facing the people, extending and then joining his hands, he says:

Priest: **Pray, brethren (brothers and sisters),**
that my sacrifice and yours
may be acceptable to God,
the almighty Father.

People: **May the Lord accept the sacrifice at your hands**
for the praise and glory of his name,
for our good and the good of all his holy Church.

Then the Priest, with hands extended, says the Prayer over the Offerings, at the end of which the people acclaim:

People: **Amen.**

THE EUCHARISTIC PRAYER

PREFACE DIALOGUE

Priest: **The Lord be with you.**

People: **And with your spirit.**

Priest: **Lift up your hearts.**

People: **We lift them up to the Lord.**

Priest: **Let us give thanks to the Lord our God.**

People: **It is right and just.**

PREFACE

It is truly right and just, our duty and our salvation, always and everywhere to give you thanks, Lord, holy Father, almighty and eternal God, through Christ our Lord.

**In him you have been pleased to renew all things,
giving us all a share in his fullness.
For though he was in the form of God, he emptied himself
and by the blood of his Cross brought peace to all creation.
Therefore he has been exalted above all things,
and to all who obey him,**

has become the source of eternal salvation.
And so, with Angels and Archangels,
with Thrones and Dominions,
and with all the hosts and Powers of heaven,
we sing the hymn of your glory,
as without end we acclaim:

Or: (COMMON PREFACE VI)

It is truly right and just, our duty and our salvation,
always and everywhere to give you thanks,
Father most holy,
through your beloved Son, Jesus Christ,
your Word through whom you made all things,
whom you sent as our Savior and Redeemer,
incarnate by the Holy Spirit and born of the Virgin.

Fulfilling your will and gaining for you a holy people,
he stretched out his hands as he endured his Passion,
so as to break the bonds of death
and manifest the resurrection.

And so, with the Angels and all the Saints
we declare your glory,
as with one voice we acclaim:

PREFACE ACCLAMATION

Holy, Holy, Holy Lord God of hosts.
Heaven and earth are full of your glory.
Hosanna in the highest.
Blessed is he who comes in the name of the Lord.
Hosanna in the highest.

EUCHARISTIC PRAYER II

You are indeed Holy, O Lord,
the fount of all holiness.
Make holy, therefore, these gifts, we pray,
by sending down your Spirit upon them like the dewfall,
so that they may become for us
the Body and ✠ Blood of our Lord Jesus Christ.
At the time he was betrayed
and entered willingly into his Passion,

He takes the bread and, holding it slightly raised above the altar, continues:

he took bread and, giving thanks, broke it,
and gave it to his disciples, saying:

He bows slightly.

TAKE THIS, ALL OF YOU, AND EAT OF IT,
FOR THIS IS MY **B**ODY,
WHICH WILL BE GIVEN UP FOR YOU.

He shows the consecrated host to the people, places it again on the paten, and genuflects in adoration. After this, he continues:

In a similar way, when supper was ended,

He takes the chalice and, holding it slightly raised above the altar, continues:

he took the chalice
and, once more giving thanks,
he gave it to his disciples, saying:

He bows slightly.

TAKE THIS, ALL OF YOU, AND DRINK FROM IT,
FOR THIS IS THE CHALICE OF MY **B**LOOD,

THE BLOOD OF THE NEW AND ETERNAL COVENANT, WHICH WILL BE POURED OUT FOR YOU AND FOR MANY FOR THE FORGIVENESS OF SINS.
DO THIS IN MEMORY OF ME.

He shows the chalice to the people, places it on the corporal, and genuflects in adoration.

MEMORIAL ACCLAMATION

Priest: **The mystery of faith.**

And the people continue, acclaiming:

People: **We proclaim your Death, O Lord,**
and profess your Resurrection
until you come again.

Or:

People: **When we eat this Bread**
and drink this Cup,
we proclaim your Death, O Lord,
until you come again.

Or:

People: **Save us, Savior of the world,**
for by your Cross and Resurrection
you have set us free.

Priest: **Therefore, as we celebrate**

the memorial of his Death and Resurrection,
we offer you, Lord,
the Bread of life and the Chalice of salvation,
giving thanks that you have held us worthy
to be in your presence and minister to you.

Humbly we pray
that, partaking of the Body and Blood of Christ,
we may be gathered into one by the Holy Spirit.

Remember, Lord, your Church,
spread throughout the world,
and bring her to the fullness of charity,
together with N. our Pope and N. our Bishop and all the clergy.

In Masses for the Dead, the following may be added:

Priest:

Remember your servant N.,
whom you have called (today)
from this world to yourself.
Grant that he (she) who was united with your Son in a death like his,
may also be one with him in his Resurrection.

Remember also our brothers and sisters
who have fallen asleep in the hope of the resurrection,
and all who have died in your mercy:
welcome them into the light of your face.
Have mercy on us all, we pray,
that with the Blessed Virgin Mary,
Mother of God,
with the blessed Apostles,

**and all the Saints who have pleased you through-
out the ages,
we may merit to be coheirs to eternal life,
and may praise and glorify you
through your Son, Jesus Christ.**

He takes the chalice and the paten with the host and, raising both, he says:

DOXOLOGY

Priest:

Through him, and with him, and in him,
O God, almighty Father,
in the unity of the Holy Spirit,
all glory and honor is yours,
for ever and ever.

People:

Amen.

THE COMMUNION RITE

After the chalice and paten have been set down, the Priest, with hands joined, says:

Priest: **At the Savior's command**
and formed by divine teaching,
we dare to say:

He extends his hands and, together with the people, continues:

Priest and People:
Our Father, who art in heaven,
hallowed be thy name;
thy kingdom come,
thy will be done
on earth as it is in heaven.
Give us this day our daily bread,
and forgive us our trespasses,
as we forgive those
who trespass against us;
and lead us not into temptation,
but deliver us from evil.

Priest: **Deliver us, Lord, we pray,**
from every evil,
graciously grant peace in our days,
that, by the help of your mercy,
we may be always free from sin
and safe from all distress,
as we await the blessed hope
and the coming of our Savior,
Jesus Christ.

People: **For the kingdom,**
the power and the glory are yours
now and for ever.

THE SIGN OF PEACE

Then the Priest, with hands extended, says aloud:

Priest: **Lord Jesus Christ,**
who said to your Apostles:
Peace I leave you, my peace I give you,
look not on our sins,
but on the faith of your Church,
and graciously grant her peace and unity
in accordance with your will.
Who live and reign for ever and ever.

People: **Amen.**

The Priest, turned towards the people, extending and then joining his hands, adds:

Priest: **The peace of the Lord**
be with you always.

People: **And with your spirit.**

Then, if appropriate, the Deacon, or the Priest, adds:

Priest: **Let us offer each other**
the sign of peace.

And all offer one another a sign, in keeping with local customs, that expresses peace, communion, and charity. The Priest gives the sign of peace to a Deacon or minister.

LAMB OF GOD

People:

Lamb of God, you take away the sins of the world,
have mercy on us.
Lamb of God, you take away the sins of the world,
have mercy on us.
Lamb of God, you take away the sins of the world,
grant us peace.

The invocation may even be repeated several times if the fraction is prolonged. Only the final time, however, is grant us peace said. Then the Priest, with hands joined, says quietly:

Priest:

Lord Jesus Christ, Son of the living God,
who, by the will of the Father
and the work of the Holy Spirit,
through your Death gave life to the world,
free me by this, your most holy Body and Blood,
from all my sins and from every evil;
keep me always faithful to your commandments,
and never let me be parted from you.

Or:

May the receiving of your Body and Blood,
Lord Jesus Christ,
not bring me to judgment and condemnation,

but through your loving mercy
be for me protection in mind and body
and a healing remedy.

The Priest genuflects, takes the host and, holding it slightly raised above the paten or above the chalice, while facing the people, says aloud:

INVITATION TO COMMUNION

Priest:

Behold the Lamb of God,
behold him who takes away the sins of the world.
Blessed are those called to the supper of the Lamb.

And together with the people he adds once:

Priest and People:

Lord, I am not worthy
that you should enter under my roof,
but only say the word
and my soul shall be healed.

COMMUNION OF THE PRIEST

Priest: **May the Body of Christ**
keep me safe for eternal life.

And he reverently consumes the Body of Christ. Then he takes the chalice and says quietly:

Priest: **May the Blood of Christ**
keep me safe for eternal life.

And he reverently consumes the Blood of Christ.

COMMUNION OF THE PEOPLE

After this, he takes the paten or ciborium and approaches the communicants. The Priest raises a host slightly and shows it to each of the communicants, saying:

Priest: **The Body of Christ.**

Communicant: **Amen.**

Then the Priest may return to the chair. If appropriate, a sacred silence may be observed for a while, or a psalm or other canticle of praise or a hymn may be sung.

Then, standing at the altar or at the chair and facing the people, with hands joined, the Priest says:

Priest: **Let us pray.**

All pray in silence with the Priest for a while, unless silence has just been observed. Then the Priest, with hands extended, says the Prayer after Communion, at the end of which the people acclaim:

People: **Amen.**

THE CONCLUDING RITE

If they are necessary, any brief announcements to the people follow here. Then the dismissal takes place. The Priest, facing the people and extending his hands, says:

FINAL BLESSING

Priest: **The Lord be with you.**

People: **And with your spirit.**

Priest: **May almighty God bless you, the Father, and the Son, ✝ and the Holy Spirit.**

People: **Amen.**

DISMISSAL

Then the Deacon, or the Priest himself, with hands joined and facing the people, says:

Deacon or Priest: **Go forth, the Mass is ended.**

Or:

Deacon or Priest: **Go and announce the Gospel of the Lord.**

Or:

Deacon or Priest: **Go in peace, glorifying the Lord by your life.**

Or:

Deacon or Priest: **Go in peace.**

People: **Thanks be to God.**

Then the Priest venerates the altar as usual with a kiss, as at the beginning. After making a profound bow with the ministers, he withdraws. If any liturgical action follows immediately, the rites of dismissal are omitted.

THE CHURCH YEAR

The seasons of the Church are: Advent, Christmas, Lent, Easter, Pentecost and Ordinary Time.

Advent means coming. Each year for four weeks before Christmas, Christians prepare their minds and hearts for the birth of Jesus.

The six weeks before Easter are called Lent. For Christians, Lent is a time of special prayer, reflection and self-denial. The first Easter was the day Jesus fulfilled His promise and arose from the dead.

Pentecost celebrates the days the disciples were gathered together and the Holy Spirit entered them. The spirit gave them the courage to be like Jesus.

During the remaining weeks, a season called Ordinary Time, the Church invites us to learn more about Jesus and His Spirit in us.

FAVORITE GOSPEL STORIES

The Gospels read at Mass are stories from the life of Jesus. They are chosen in accordance with the seasons of the Church Year. The Gospels rotate on a three year schedule: Cycle A, Cycle B and Cycle C.

The following selection is a brief introduction to the Church's large number of Gospels. Read these and other stories from the New Testament as often as you can.

Always be attentive and listen carefully during Mass. The more Gospel stories you read and hear, the closer you will be drawn to Jesus; He will send the Holy Spirit to fill your heart with love and wisdom.

AN ANGEL SPEAKS TO MARY

Matthew 1:18–25; Luke 1:26–38

In Nazareth, there lived a young woman named Mary, who was engaged to Joseph, a carpenter, and an angel of the Lord came to her with a message. "Do not be afraid, Mary," said the angel. God has sent me to tell you that you will be the mother of a son, and His name will be Jesus."

Mary was surprised, but the angel said, "The Holy Spirit will come to you, and your child shall be called the Son of God. He shall rule a kingdom that will last forever."

Mary said, "I am God's servant. I will do what He asks." Then the angel went away.

JESUS IS BORN

Luke 2:1–20

In time Mary and Joseph, her husband, went to Bethlehem, but the town was crowded and they had to sleep in a cave. Mary's baby, Jesus, was born there that night.

Nearby an angel came to some shepherds who were watching their sheep, and he said, "A child has been born in Bethlehem. He is Christ the Lord." Many angels sang:

"Glory to God in the highest,
and peace on earth."

The shepherds went to Bethlehem to see the child and they found Him with Mary and Joseph. Then the shepherds went away praising God.

THE CHILD JESUS IN THE TEMPLE

Luke 2:41–52

After a holiday, Mary and Joseph were returning home to Nazareth with their friends and twelve-year-old Jesus. At first Mary thought Jesus was with another family, but when she learned He was not, she and Joseph went back to Jerusalem to look for Him. They searched for three days before they found Him in the temple. He was talking with teachers who were amazed at His knowledge of God's teachings.

Mary asked, "Son, why have you worried us so?" Jesus answered, "Didn't you know that I must do My Father's work?" However, He went home with Mary and Joseph and obeyed them.

JESUS SPEAKS TO THE PEOPLE

Matthew 5:1–12, 6:5–15; Luke 6:17–26, 11:1–5

One day Jesus went to a mountain top, and He spoke to the people. He said, "Love everyone, even those who are not kind to you. Treat others as you want them to treat you. Ask God your Father for whatever you need. Here is how you are to pray to Him:

"Our father Who art in heaven, hallowed be Thy name. Thy kingdom come; Thy will be done on earth as it is in heaven. Give us this day our daily bread, and forgive us our trespasses, as we forgive those who trespass against us, and lead us not into temptation, but deliver us from evil."

A STORM ON THE LAKE

Matthew 8:23–27; Mark 4:35–41; Luke 8:22–25

One evening Jesus said to His Apostles, "Let us sail to the other side of the lake." When their boat was out on the water, a storm arose. Winds blew and waves beat against the sides of the little vessel, but Jesus had fallen asleep.

The Apostles woke Him and cried, "Master save us or we shall drown!" Jesus stood and said to the sea, "Peace. Be still." At once the winds fell and the sea grew calm. Jesus asked the Apostles, "Why were you afraid?" They said to one another, "Who is this Jesus? Even the wind and the waves obey Him."

JESUS FEEDS THE PEOPLE

Matthew 14:13–21; Mark 6:34–44;
Luke 9:10–17; John 6:1–15

A crowd had followed Jesus all day, and in the evening the Apostles said, "The people are hungry." The Apostle Philip announced, "A boy is here with five loaves of bread and two fishes, but that is not enough for so many." Jesus said, "Let the people sit down." After the five thousand were seated on the grass, Jesus blessed the loaves and fishes, and the Apostles handed them to the crowd. When everyone had eaten, they picked up what was left, and the food filled twelve baskets. The people were amazed that Jesus had fed so many with so little food.

THE LOVING FATHER

Luke 15:11–32

A young man left home and went to live in a far place where he spent his money foolishly. When it was all gone, he took a job caring for pigs, but the pigs had more to eat than he had, and he said, "The men who work for my father always have enough food. I will go home and ask if I may work for him." He walked along and when his father saw him, he ran to the son and kissed him. The son said, "Father, I am not worthy to be your son," but the father said to a servant, "Prepare a feast so that we may celebrate my son's return home."

JESUS CURES A BLIND MAN

John 9:1–41

When Jesus saw a blind man begging at the side of a road, He put clay on the blind man's eyes and told him to go and wash it off. The man obeyed and at once he was able to see. His parents were amazed, for they knew their son had been born blind and had been that way all his life.

Not long after, Jesus again met the man who had been born blind and asked him, "Do you believe in the Son of God?" The man said, "Who is He? Tell me and I will believe in Him." Jesus said, "It is I. You are looking at God's Son." Then the man knelt down and worshiped Him.

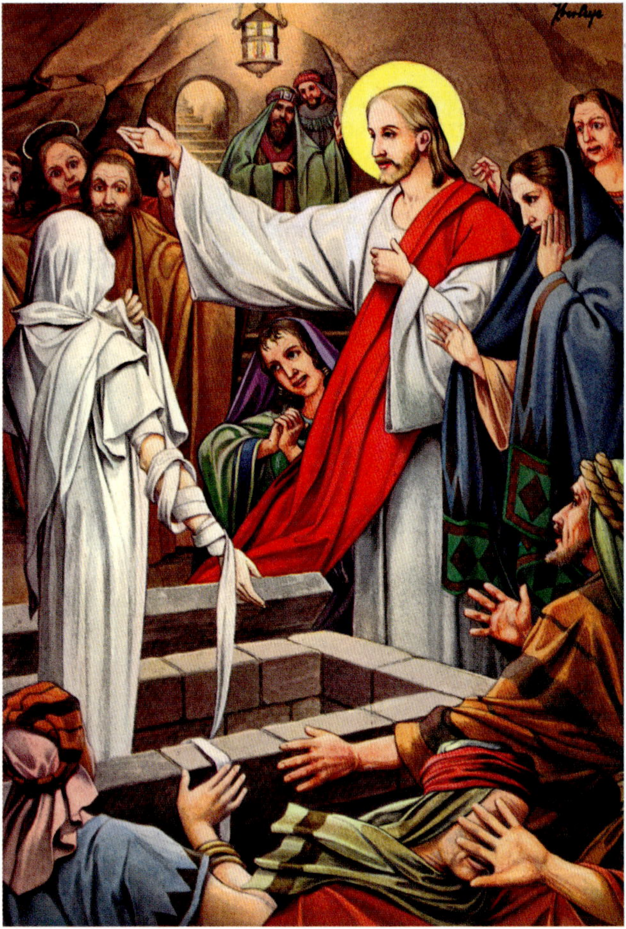

THE RAISING OF LAZARUS

John 11:1–44

When Jesus heard that His friend Lazarus had died, He went to visit the dead man's sisters. One of them, Mary, said to Jesus, "If You had been here, Lazarus would not have died."

Jesus said, "Let us go to the cave where he is buried." When they reached it, Jesus said, "Take away the stone that closes the cave." Then He prayed, "Father in heaven, do what I ask You today so that those who are standing here will know it was You Who sent Me." Then He cried, "Lazarus, come out of the tomb." At once the man who had been dead got up and walked out to his friends.

JESUS ENTERS JERUSALEM

Matthew 21:1–11; Mark 11:1; Luke 19:28–38; John 12:12–19

When Jesus was near Jerusalem, two of His friends brought Him a young donkey, and Jesus sat upon it to ride into the city. Many people threw their coats on the road in front of Him, and others cut branches from trees and cast them in His path to show their love for Jesus. Then those who marched before Him began to praise God for the wonderful things Jesus had done for them and for all He had taught them. They shouted:

"Blessed is He Who comes as king
in the name of the Lord!
Hosanna to the Son of David!
Glory in the highest!"

THE LAST SUPPER

Matthew 26:17–30; Mark 14:12–26; Luke 22:14–20

On Holy Thursday, Jesus washed the feet of His Apostles and then sat down to eat supper with them. During the meal, He took the bread and gave it to the Apostles and said, "Take this and eat; it is My body." Then He took a cup of wine and said, "Drink this; it is My blood."

He said to His Apostles, "Love one another as I love you. Soon I will leave you to go to My Father, but I will send the Holy Spirit Who will live with you and teach you what you need to know."

Then Jesus and the Apostles sang a hymn and prayed together.

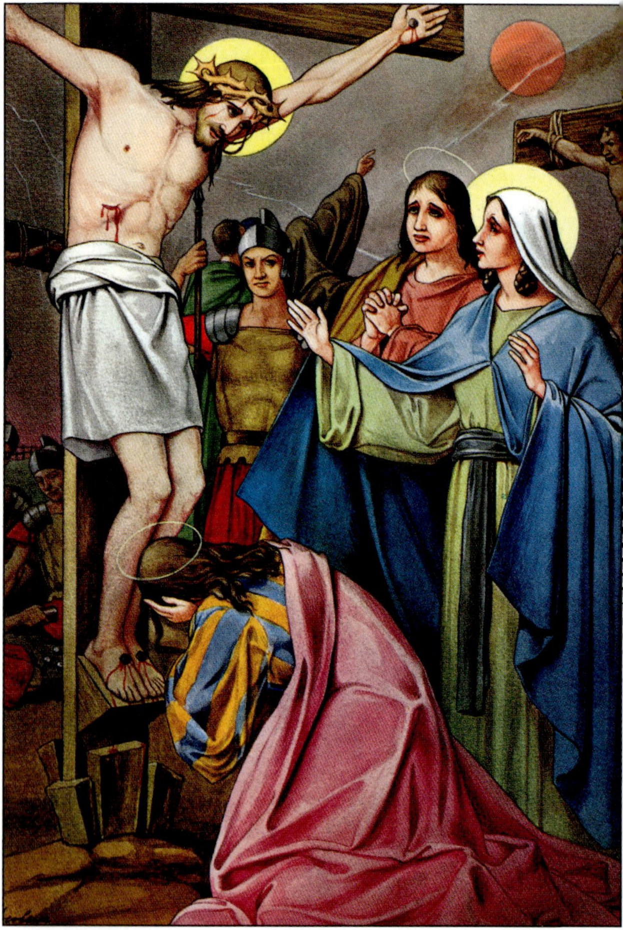

JESUS IS PUT TO DEATH

Matthew 26:1–75, 27:1–66; Mark 14:1–72, 15:1–47; Luke 22:1–71, 23:1–56; John 18:1–40, 19:1–42

Men in power hated Jesus because He had said He was the Son of God. Now Judas, one of the Apostles, did an evil act. He told the enemies of Jesus where to find Him, and on Holy Thursday they arrested Him. When the judges asked Him if He were truly the Son of God, Jesus would not deny it. Then He was flogged, and soldiers put a crown of thorns on His head because the people had called Him their king.

On Good Friday, Jesus was taken to Golgotha and nailed to a cross, and there He died. His friends took down His body, wrapped it in a sheet, and buried it in a cave.

EASTER

Matthew 28:1–10; Mark 16:1–11; Luke 24:1–12; John 20:1–18

On Easter morning, some women went to the tomb where Jesus lay to put spices on His body. Suddenly they remembered that a heavy stone had been rolled in front of the tomb. One woman said, "Who will roll away the stone for us?" However, when they got there it had already been rolled away, and a man in white robes was sitting in the tomb. He said, "Do not be afraid. Jesus has risen from the dead. Tell Peter and the other Apostles." As the women ran off, they saw Jesus, and they knelt to adore Him. He said, "Tell the Apostles to wait for Me in Galilee."

THE APOSTLES SEE THE RISEN JESUS

Matthew 28:16–20; Mark 16:12–18; Luke 24:36–49; John 20:19–31

The Apostles were indoors when Jesus came to them and said, "Peace be with you." He showed them His wounded hands, but Thomas, one of the Apostles, was not there. When they told him they had seen Jesus, he said, "I do not believe it. If I can put my fingers in His wounds, I will believe He is risen."

Again Jesus came, and when He saw Thomas He said, "Put your fingers into My wounds." However, Thomas said, "My Lord and my God." And Jesus said, "You believe because you see Me. Blessed are people who do not see Me and who believe."

THE ASCENSION

Mark 16:19–20; Luke 24:50–53; Acts 1:6–12

After Jesus rose from the dead, He stayed on earth for forty days, visiting His Apostles and talking to them. He said to them, "Go and teach all people what I have taught you, but wait in Jerusalem until I send you the Holy Spirit." After that, Jesus led them to Mount Olivet and blessed them. Then He rose slowly toward the sky until a cloud hid Him from sight. As they kept looking up two men in white appeared and said, "Men of Galilee, why do you stand gazing up at the sky? Jesus, Who has gone to heaven, will return again." Then the Apostles went back to Jerusalem.

THE COMING OF THE HOLY SPIRIT

Acts 2:1–13

The Apostles, Mary, the mother of Jesus, and their friends prayed and waited for the coming of the Holy Spirit. Then, one day, they heard a sound like the wind, and tongues of fire settled on them. All were filled with the Holy Spirit and they began to speak in many languages. Now visitors from other lands were in Jerusalem, and when the Apostles began to speak, the visitors said, "How is it that, no matter what countries we come from, we hear the Apostles speaking in our own languages?" The Apostles told the story of God's son and great numbers believed in Jesus and became His followers.

RECONCILIATION

Jesus has asked us to love God with all our heart, all our mind and all our soul; and to love our neighbor as ourself.

Sometimes we do not follow Jesus and we fail to love as we should. This separates us from God. It is the way we sin.

But Jesus loves us too much to let us remain apart. He wants very much to forgive us if only we go to Him, say we are sorry and promise to do better. This we do through the Sacrament of Reconciliation.

EXAMINATION OF CONSCIENCE

Before confessing your sins, it is important to look at your life and ask yourself some questions:

Have I behaved as God's child
should?
Do I pray to God every day?
Have I given trouble to my
parents and teachers?
Have I been selfish in my
dealings with others?
Have I been honest and truthful?
Have I quarreled and not tried to
make friends again?
Have I neglected my work in
school or at home?
Do I respect my body and take
good care of it?
Do I help those who are poor or
handicapped or have other needs?

Do I show the old, the sick or the
lonely that I care about them?

When going to confession, either in the Reconciliation Room or behind the confessional screen, always remember that the priest represents Jesus. There is no need to be afraid. The priest is there to help you. He will show you how to let Jesus come into your life.

RECEIVING THE SACRAMENT

After you greet the priest, make the Sign of the Cross. The priest may read a passage from Holy Scripture. If he does, listen carefully to God's Word.

You will then speak to the priest about your sins. Tell him whatever is keeping you away from God and preventing you from being a better follower of Jesus.

When you are finished, the priest will counsel you and may ask you to say a prayer or do something to show your sorrow. He may ask you to recite an Act of Contrition.

ACT OF CONTRITION

O my God, I am heartily sorry for having offended You and I detest all my sins, because of Your just punishments, but most of all because they offend You, my God, Who is all good and deserving of all my love. I firmly resolve, with the help of Your grace, to sin no more and to avoid the near occasions of sin. Amen.

Then the priest will say the words of absolution and reconciliation.

When you leave, remember to thank the priest. Then remain a few minutes in church and tell Jesus how happy and grateful you are because your sins are forgiven.

I.N.R.I.

THE STATIONS OF THE CROSS

Each Good Friday, we recall the passion of Jesus, the day He suffered and died on the cross.

On the first Good Friday, almost 2000 years ago, Jesus made many stops on the way to Calvary. The fourteen pictures around the walls of our church remind us of all that happened on that sad day.

A good way to thank Jesus is to visit each station, think of what happened and tell Jesus how much we love Him.

First Station
JESUS MEETS PILATE

Jesus' first stop on the way of the cross is the Governor's palace. Many Jewish leaders wanted Jesus out of the way. "Crucify Him," they insisted, and they influenced Pilate the Governor to condemn Jesus to death.

Second Station
JESUS TAKES THE CROSS

The Roman soldiers bring a large wooden cross for Jesus to carry. It is very heavy and rough. Though Jesus is tired, sick, and weak, He reaches out and accepts the cross lovingly. By His love He transforms this cross into a symbol of hope and salvation for all people.

Third Station
JESUS FALLS

Soon after He begins to carry the cross, Jesus falls. He is very exhausted and the weight of the cross crushes Him. The soldiers roughly drag Him to His feet and Jesus slowly continues His painful journey.

Fourth Station
JESUS MEETS HIS MOTHER

On the narrow roadway, Jesus turns the corner and looks ahead to see His mother. She reaches out to touch Him. He is thankful that she is there. She doesn't say anything to Him, but He knows that she loves Him even though she feels sad and helpless to do anything.

Fifth Station

SIMON HELPS JESUS

The soldiers notice that Jesus is very weak. He is staggering under the load, so they pull a man from the crowd, a stranger, and force him to help Jesus carry His cross. The stranger, whose name is Simon Cyrene, is frightened and doesn't know Who Jesus is.

Sixth Station

VERONICA WIPES JESUS' FACE

A woman named Veronica steps out from the crowd with a towel. Jesus' hands are holding His cross, so she wipes His face, which is dripping with blood and sweat. Veronica does a simple act of kindness to show she cares.

Seventh Station

JESUS FALLS AGAIN

The soldiers let Simon go his way and Jesus is again carrying the cross by Himself. There is still a long way to go. Jesus staggers and falls. He is breathing very heavily and has no strength left. Yet He stands up, and because of His strong love, He is able to go forward.

Eighth Station

JESUS MEETS SOME WOMEN

Jesus meets a group of women from Jerusalem. They are weeping because He is suffering so much. Jesus tells them to weep for themselves and for their children because the cruelty in the world will surely touch them just as it is touching Him.

Ninth Station

JESUS FALLS A THIRD TIME

A third time Jesus falls. He has no more strength left. He has lost much blood and the hot sun burns His skin. Again He struggles to stand up because He has chosen the way of the cross out of love for us.

Tenth Station

JESUS IS STRIPPED

Jesus has reached the top of the hill. The soldiers let Him drop the cross to the ground. And while Jesus stands there in front of the crowds, the soldiers pull off His clothes leaving Him embarrassed and humiliated. He is being treated as a common criminal, as if He were a worthless human being.

Eleventh Station

JESUS IS NAILED TO THE CROSS

Now the soldiers make Jesus lie down on the cross. They stretch out His arms and fasten them with nails. They also nail His feet so that He is securely fastened to the cross. He cannot escape. Only His great love for us enables Jesus to bear His pain and suffering.

Twelfth Station

JESUS DIES

The cross is standing and Jesus is hanging on it. Time goes by very slowly, for Jesus is full of pain, but more important than the pain is His love for us and His willingness to die for us to be free from sin.

Thirteenth Station
JESUS IS PLACED IN MARY'S ARMS

After Jesus dies, a few friends gently take His body down from the cross and put it in the arms of His mother. She held Jesus like this when He was a baby, but now His body has no life left in it. Her heart is filled with sadness.

Fourteenth Station
JESUS IS BURIED

The final stopping place for Jesus on this sad day is a tomb. His friends place His body on the stone slab, wipe off the blood, wash His body clean, and cover it with cloth and nice-smelling spices. His friends and His mother touch His body for the last time before they leave.

A HAPPY ENDING

After we recall the Fourteen Stations, it is good to remember what follows Good Friday. Jesus' story does not end in sadness but in joy. He not only died, but on Easter Sunday He rose out of His tomb gloriously alive.

Jesus' Father, Who is God, willed to allow Jesus to die out of love for us. He also willed to bring Jesus back to life so that in Jesus we would have no fear of death. Jesus will lead us through death to new life.

THE ROSARY

The rosary is a special way of praying to God that honors Mary, the Mother of Jesus. While reciting prayers, you think about certain stories in the lives of Jesus and Mary. These stories are called mysteries: a mystery is a story about God.

Rosary beads are used to keep count of the prayers and mysteries. Recite the Apostles' Creed while you hold the crucifix, then one Our Father and three Hail Marys. After that, as you think about each mystery, recite the Our Father on the large bead, the Hail Mary on each of ten smaller beads and finish with a Glory Be. That makes one decade. The complete rosary consists of five decades. There are four sets of mysteries and five stories in each set of mysteries.

THE JOYFUL MYSTERIES

Mondays and Saturdays and Sundays of the Christmas season

1. The Coming of Jesus Is Announced
2. Mary Visits Elizabeth
3. Jesus Is Born
4. Jesus Is Presented to God
5. Jesus Is Found in the Temple

THE MYSTERIES OF LIGHT

Thursdays

1. Jesus' Baptism in the Jordan
2. The Wedding at Cana
3. Jesus' Proclamation of God's Kingdom
4. Jesus' Transfiguration
5. Jesus' Institution of the Eucharist

THE SORROWFUL MYSTERIES

Tuesdays and Fridays and Sundays of the Lenten Season

1. Jesus' Agony in the Garden
2. Jesus Is Whipped
3. Jesus Is Crowned with Thorns
4. Jesus Carries His Cross
5. Jesus Dies on the Cross

THE GLORIOUS MYSTERIES

Wednesdays and Sundays

1. Jesus Rises from His Tomb
2. Jesus Ascends to Heaven
3. The Holy Spirit Descends
4. Mary Is Assumed into Heaven
5. Mary Is Crowned in Heaven

THE SACRAMENTS

Christ instituted seven sacraments. They are outward visible signs of God's grace given at special moments in a person's life. They help us live our lives more fully.

BAPTISM

Baptism is also called christening. It is the first sacrament we receive, and makes us members of the church. It is performed by pouring water on a person's forehead, and saying "I baptize you in the name of the Father, and of the Son, and of the Holy Spirit. Amen."

CONFIRMATION

Confirmation bestows the special seal or mark of the Holy Spirit. It gives you the special spiritual energy to make Jesus known in the world, and the courage to live the way Jesus would like you to live.

HOLY EUCHARIST

Communion is often called the greatest sacrament because Christ Himself is present in the consecrated bread and wine. The bread and wine are transformed into Christ's body and blood by the priest during Mass.

RECONCILIATION

This sacrament brings us God's forgiveness through the words of a priest. Reconciliation makes us holy and reconciles us with God and the Church. This used to be called "Penance" or "Confession."

ANOINTING OF THE SICK

This sacrament is for the seriously ill, the infirm and the very old. The sacrament of the sick sanctifies sufferings, increases grace, forgives sins and makes us ready for heaven.

HOLY ORDERS

This sacrament gives priests the power to forgive sins, the power to anoint the sick, the power to change bread and wine into the body and blood of Christ, and the power to perpetuate Jesus' sacrifice, which is the Mass. Through Holy Orders, priests and bishops receive the Spirit's grace to guide the church and take care of the people of God.

MATRIMONY

This sacrament is received when a husband and wife pronounce their marriage vows. It gives the grace for two people to join their lives together until death. The husband and wife perform this sacrament for each other. The priest is only the official church witness of this sacrament. Matrimony also enables people to be good mothers and fathers.

THE TEN COMMANDMENTS

1. I am the Lord your God. You shall not have strange gods before Me.
2. You shall not take the Name of the Lord your God in vain.
3. Remember to keep holy the Lord's Day.
4. Honor your father and your mother.
5. You shall not kill.
6. You shall not commit adultery.
7. You shall not steal.
8. You shall not bear false witness against your neighbor.
9. You shall not covet your neighbor's wife.
10. You shall not covet your neighbor's goods.

THE PRECEPTS OF THE CHURCH

1. To attend Mass every Sunday and holy day of obligation.
2. To celebrate the Sacrament of Reconciliation at least once a year and to receive Holy Communion during Easter time.
3. To study Catholic teaching in preparation for the Sacrament of Confirmation and then to continue our religious education.
4. To observe the marriage laws of the Church.
5. To strengthen and support the Church.
6. To do penance, including abstaining and fasting on the appointed days.
7. To join in the missionary spirit and apostolate of the Church.

MEMORY PRAYERS

To pray is to talk to God or to think about Him. Sometimes we pray in our own words and tell what is deep in our hearts. Other times we say the prayers known by all Catholics. Some of these prayers are listed below. You should memorize them so you can say them at any time of the day or night.

THE SIGN OF THE CROSS

In the name of the Father
and of the Son †
and of the Holy Spirit.
Amen.

THE GLORY BE

Glory be to the Father, and to the Son, and to the Holy Spirit, as it was in the beginning, is now, and ever shall be, world without end. Amen.

THE OUR FATHER

Our Father, Who art in heaven, hallowed be Thy name; Thy kingdom come; Thy will be done on earth as it is in heaven. Give us this day our daily bread, and forgive us our trespasses as we forgive those who trespass against us and lead us not into temptation, but deliver us from evil. Amen.

THE HAIL MARY

Hail Mary, full of grace, the Lord is with thee. Blessed art thou amongst women, and blessed is the fruit of thy womb, Jesus. Holy Mary, Mother of God, pray for us sinners, now and at the hour of our death. Amen.

THE APOSTLES' CREED

I believe in God,
the Father almighty,
Creator of heaven and earth,
and in Jesus Christ, his only Son, our Lord,

At the words that follow, up to and including the Virgin Mary, *all bow*

who was conceived by the Holy Spirit,
born of the Virgin Mary,
suffered under Pontius Pilate,
was crucified, died and was buried;
he descended into hell;
on the third day he rose again from the dead;
he ascended into heaven,
and is seated at the right hand of God the Father almighty;
from there he will come to judge the living and the dead.

I believe in the Holy Spirit,
the holy catholic Church,
the communion of saints,
the forgiveness of sins,
the resurrection of the body,
and life everlasting. Amen.

GRACE BEFORE MEALS

Bless us, O Lord, and these Your gifts, which we are about to receive from Your goodness, through Christ our Lord. Amen.

or:

We thank You, O Lord, for these gifts and for all the gifts we have received from Your goodness, through Christ our Lord. Amen.

THE "MEMORARE"

Remember, O most gracious Virgin Mary, that never was it known that anyone who fled to your protection, implored your help or sought your intercession, was left unaided. Inspired with this confidence, I fly to you, O Virgin of virgins, my Mother; to you do I come, before you I stand, sinful and sorrowful. O Mother of the Word Incarnate, despise not my petitions, but in your mercy hear and answer me. Amen.

PRAYER TO THE HOLY SPIRIT

Come, O Holy Spirit, fill the hearts of Your faithful and kindle in them the fire of Your love.

V. Send forth Your Spirit
and they shall be created

R. And You shall renew
the face of the earth.

Let us pray:
O God, who has taught the hearts of the faithful by the light of the Holy Spirit, grant that in the same Spirit, we may be always truly wise and ever rejoice in His consolation. Through Christ our Lord. Amen.

SOUL OF CHRIST

(This is a prayer of Saint Ignatius Loyola.)

Soul of Christ, sanctify me.
Body of Christ, save me.
Blood of Christ, inebriate me.
Water from the side of Christ,
    wash me.
Passion of Christ, strengthen me.
O good Jesus, hear me.
Within Your wounds, hide me.
Separated from You,
    let me never be.
From the malignant enemy,
    defend me.
At the hour of death, call me.
To come to You, bid me,
    that I may praise You
    in the company of Your saints,
    for all eternity. Amen.

MORNING PRAYER

Dear God, I thank You for watching over me during the night. Today I offer You my whole self: my every thought, word and act. Please keep me from harm. Bless my parents, my family and everyone I love.

EVENING PRAYER

Dear God, before I go to bed, please hear my last prayer. Thank You for all Your help today. Forgive me any wrong I did. I am truly sorry. Keep in Your care, my mother and father, and everyone I love. May the souls of the faithful departed, through the mercy of God, rest in peace. Amen.

A VISIT TO CHURCH

It is most pleasing to God when we make a visit to Church and speak to Jesus quietly and alone.

If we do this often, we shall grow very close to our Lord and His grace will be with us to guide our every moment.

In addition to our words and thoughts, the following prayers may be said:

ACT OF FAITH

O my God, I believe that You are one God in three Divine Persons: Father, Son and Holy Spirit. I believe that Your Divine Son became Man and died for our sins, and that He will come again to judge the living and the dead. I believe these and all the truths that the Catholic Church teaches, because You have revealed them, who can neither deceive nor be deceived. Amen.

ACT OF HOPE

O my God, relying on Your almighty power and infinite mercy and promises, I hope to obtain pardon of my sins, the help of Your grace and life everlasting through the merits of Jesus Christ, my Lord and Redeemer. Amen.

ACT OF LOVE

O my God, I love You above all things with my whole heart and soul, because You are all good and worthy of all my love. I love my neighbor as myself for the love of You. I forgive all who have injured me and ask pardon of all whom I have injured. Amen.

THE BEATITUDES

1. Blessed are the poor in spirit, for the kingdom of heaven is theirs.
2. Blessed are those who are sad, for they shall be comforted.
3. Blessed are the mild and gentle, for they shall inherit the land.
4. Blessed are those who hunger and thirst for justice, for they shall be filled.
5. Blessed are the merciful, for they shall receive mercy.
6. Blessed are the pure in heart, for they shall see God.
7. Blessed are those who make peace, for they shall be called the children of God.
8. Blessed are those who suffer for My sake, for heaven will be theirs.

THE CHIEF SPIRITUAL WORKS OF MERCY

To admonish the sinner.
To instruct the ignorant.
To counsel the doubtful.
To comfort the sorrowful.
To bear wrongs patiently.
To forgive all injuries.
To pray for the living and the dead.

THE CHIEF CORPORAL WORKS OF MERCY

To feed the hungry.
To give drink to the thirsty.
To clothe the naked.
To visit the imprisoned.
To shelter the homeless.
To visit the sick.
To bury the dead.

GUARDIAN ANGEL PRAYER

Angel of God
my Guardian dear
to whom God's love
commits me here.
Ever this day
be at my side
to light and guard
to rule and guide.
Amen.

MY OWN PRAYER FOR THIS SPECIAL DAY

MY OWN PRAYER FOR MY FRIENDS

MY OWN PRAYER FOR MY FAMILY

MY OWN PRAYER TO MY FAVORITE SAINT

PERSONAL RECORD

Name ______________________________

born ________________ **in** ______________

Baptism

Date ______________________________

Priest ______________________________

Parish ______________________________

Godfather ______________________________

Godmother ______________________________

First Communion

Date ______________________________

Priest ______________________________

Parish ______________________________

Confirmation

Date ______________________________

Bishop ______________________________

Parish ______________________________

Sponsor ______________________________

Confirmation name ____________________

FAMILY RECORD

Father______________________________

born____________________ **in**________________

Mother______________________________

born____________________ **in**________________

Brothers and Sisters__________________

____

____

Father's Family

Grandfather______________________________

born__________________________________

Grandmother____________________________

born__________________________________

Mother's Family

Grandfather______________________________

born__________________________________

Grandmother____________________________

born__________________________________

INRI

PRAYER BEFORE A CRUCIFIX

Look down upon me, good and gentle Jesus, while I kneel and ask You to fill my heart with faith, hope, charity and true sorrow for my sins. Help me never to sin again.

I think of Your five wounds with great love and pity as I repeat the words of Your prophet, David, "They have pierced my hands and my feet; they have injured all my bones."

(Say one Our Father, Hail Mary, and Glory Be, for the Pope.)

"I will be with you
all Days,

Even until the End of time."